Giving expression to
the events that
punctuate life . . .

To:

_____

From:

_____

Date:

_____

humor for the lighter side of life

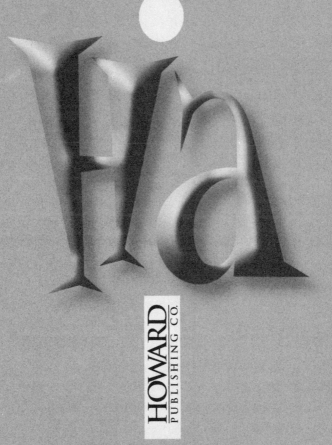

HOWARD PUBLISHING CO.

Martha Bolton

the exclamat!on series

Our purpose at Howard Publishing is to:
•*Increase faith* in the hearts of growing Christians
•*Inspire holiness* in the lives of believers
•*Instill hope* in the hearts of struggling people everywhere
Because He's coming again!

Ha! © 2006 by Martha Bolton
All rights reserved. Printed in the United States of America
Published by Howard Publishing Co., Inc.
3117 North Seventh Street, West Monroe, LA 71291-2227
www.howardpublishing.com

06 07 08 09 10 11 12 13 14 15   10 9 8 7 6 5 4 3 2 1

Edited by Between the Lines
Interior design by Stephanie D. Walker and Tennille Paden
Illustrations by Rex Bohn

Library of Congress Cataloging-in-Publication Data

Ha! : humor for the lighter side of life / [complied by] Martha Bolton
        p. cm. — (The exclamation series)
    ISBN 1-58229-479-8
    1. Quotations, English. 2. Wit and humor. I. Bolton, Martha, 1951-II Series.

PN6084.H8H36 2005
082'.02'07—dc22

                                                                2005052738

Scripture quotations are taken from the *Holy Bible, New International Version* ®. Copyright © 1973, 1978, 1984 by International Bible Society. Used by permission of Zondervan Publishing House. All rights reserved. Scripture quotations marked The Message are taken from *The Message*. Copyright © 1993, 1994, 1995, 1996, 2000, 2001, 2002. Used by permission of NavPress Publishing Group. All rights reserved.

"The Raven-ing" is reprinted from *Cooking with Hot Flashes* (Bethany House), used with permission. "Just So You Know . . . Middle-Age Fashion Faux Pas" is reprinted from *Didn't My Skin Used to Fit?* (Martha Bolton, Bethany House, a division of Baker Publishing Group, © 2000), used with permission. "You might be a workaholic if . . ." is reprinted from *Still the One* (Revell), used with permission. Portions of "You know it's time to clean house when . . ." are reprinted from *Don't Wake Me 'til after Lunch* (Revell), used with permission. "You know it's time to go home when . . ." is reprinted from *When the Meatloaf Explodes, It's Done* (Beacon Hill Press), used with permission.

Contents

contents

Part Two: The Power of *Ha!*

Introduction to *Ha!*

Total absence of humor renders life impossible.

Colette

You've gotta laugh. Far too many things in life are embarrassing, unexpected, stressful, irritating, confusing, ridiculous, and frustrating not to laugh at least about some of them.

Besides, a good *Ha!* is healthy. It's been said that a hearty laugh can burn off up to thirty-five calories. I don't know about you, but to me that sounds a whole lot better than running in a marathon or working out on a treadmill. (My pillow keeps getting stuck in the conveyor belt anyway.)

They say laughter gets our hearts beating faster, too, bringing more oxygen into our bodies. Laughing has even been credited with releasing chemicals into our bloodstream that can actually make us feel better.

Whether laughter can ward off serious illness, prolong life, or increase immunity, only the medical community can say for sure. But laughing can certainly help give us a better outlook on life. Just think of the last time you watched a comedy that made you laugh out loud. Afterward, did you find yourself thinking about your problems, or were you happily replaying the funniest scenes in your mind, maybe even passing along the humor to others?

What about after you visited with that lifelong friend and laughed most of the night away? Did you think about your aching back even once while you were sharing a belly laugh? You might have said, "Stop, stop; it hurts!" but you have said you didn't really want the fun to stop,

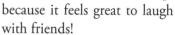

because it feels great to laugh with friends!

And that's another by-product of laughter—friends. People with a healthy sense of humor just seem to have more friends. Fun people attract fun people. I'd much rather surround myself with positive, fun-loving people than with nitpicking ol' grouches, wouldn't you?

When I was a teenager, one of my favorite poems began, "Laugh, and the world laughs with you." I even memorized it and would often recite it to myself whenever I started feeling down. I believed the words of that poem back then, and I still do today. Happy people can't help but attract other happy people.

But being happy doesn't mean we don't have any hurts to endure or that we're in denial about the difficult situations we have to cope with. We all have our share of hurtful experiences. We all have valleys to walk through. But the strange and amazing truth is, often the people with the most problems are the happiest. Maybe that's because they know firsthand the importance of laughter. They've learned not to let the stress of today rob them of their joy. They have discovered life's secret weapon, and it's called humor. It helps us cope. It gives us hope. The simple truth is, we can't make it through this stressful, irritating, full-of-surprises life without plenty of *Ha!*

Life's too important to be taken seriously.

Oscar Wilde

Introduction to *Ha!*

I have learned from experience that the greater part of our happiness or misery depends on our dispositions and not on our circumstances.

Martha Washington

It's Your Choice!

Laugh or cry
Grin or growl
Shine or whine
Smile or scowl

Smirk or bark
Joke or jeer
Whoop or snarl
Jest or sneer

It's your choice
Which to embrace
But only smiles
Improve your face

A positive attitude may not solve all your problems, but it will annoy enough people to make it worth the effort.

Herm Albright

It is requisite for the relaxation of the mind that we make use, from time to time, of playful deeds and jokes.

Saint Thomas Aquinas

Mix a little foolishness with your serious plans. It is lovely to be silly at the right moment.

Horace

The Constitution only guarantees the
American people the right to pursue happiness.
You have to catch it yourself.

Benjamin Franklin

Celebrating the *Ha!*

Uh-Oh!
The *Hal* of Embarrassment

Nobody in the game of football should be called a genius. A genius is someone like Norman Einstein.

Joe Theisman

Sometimes humor comes from embarrassing moments. Once, while shopping in an off-Broadway shoe store, I was tempted to try on a pair of UGG-like boots. I really just wanted to see how I would look in them, not necessarily buy a pair. I looked through the boxes and finally found a pair my size. I looked around for one of those benches to sit on, but there weren't any in my aisle. The aisle did happen to be lined with jumbo boxes of shoes, so I figured I would just sit on one of the boxes. As I did, I discovered that the box was empty, and down I went, all the way to the bottom. I was now stuck in the box, wedged tightly between the cardboard with my feet sticking up in the air. I felt like the filling in a taco.

I couldn't raise myself up, so I decided to rock back and forth to try to get the box to tip over. After rocking for a little while, inadvertently keeping time with the music playing on the overhead speakers, I finally got the box on its side and wrestled my way to freedom. The security officers are probably still passing around that surveillance video.

Embarrassing moments happen to all of us. We take embarrassing tumbles (mine was down the stairs at a Broadway production of *Les Miserables*), wear our clothes inside out or with the tags still on them, say the wrong thing, do the wrong thing, forget people's names that we should know, spill food on ourselves, and endure countless other incidents that can drive us into temporary hiding—or, better yet, provide plenty of laughter for years to come.

Humor is just another defense
against the universe.

Mel Brooks

An attorney meets Saint Peter at the gates and tries to convince him that there must have been some mistake. His time can't be up yet.

Saint Peter replies, "Oh, there is no mistake, sir. We reviewed the number of hours you've billed your clients for, and by our estimation you're 196 years old."

Unknown

Man does not live by words alone, despite the fact that sometimes he has to eat them.

Adlai E. Stevenson

Wit makes its own welcome, and levels all distinctions. No dignity, no learning, no force of character, can make any stand against good wit.

Ralph Waldo Emerson

Oh-Me!

The *Hal* of Laughing at Yourself

You grow up the day you have the
first real laugh at yourself.

Ethel Barrymore

The main reason we should laugh at ourselves is simply
that we supply ourselves with an endless source of material. Who else do we know as well as we know ourselves?
Who else can watch our every move so intently and compare our hopes of what we wanted to happen with the

reality of what did happen? Maybe we wanted to enter the room as discreetly as possible, but instead we tripped and tumbled our way in. Maybe we wanted to make a good impression on the boss at the office banquet and hadn't planned on getting that leaf of spinach stuck between our teeth quite as prominently as it did.

We don't intend for things to go wrong, but often they do. And if we don't laugh at ourselves every chance we get, we're wasting a lot of great material. We're also missing out on a lot of personal growth. Ethel Barrymore was right. When we can laugh at ourselves, when we have a good, self-aimed *Ha!* it really is a sign of maturity. It means we've let go of the unrealistic demand for perfection, either self-imposed or placed on us by other people, and instead, we've decided to have a good laugh and move on.

Laughter won't erase our imperfections. It just makes them a little easier to handle. It won't take away our failures, but it will give us a more solid footing on which to begin again. And if we don't go a little easier on ourselves, who will?

When I was a kid, we used to play a game called Spin the Bottle. If the bottle pointed to you, the girl could either kiss you or give you a nickel. By the time I was thirteen, I owned my own home.

Gene Perret

I have been described as a lighthouse in the middle of a bog: brilliant but useless.

Conor Cruise O'Brien

The embarrassing thing is that the salad dressing is out-grossing my films.

Paul Newman

I was called "Rembrandt" Hope in my boxing days because I spent so much time on the canvas.

Bob Hope

If you would not be laughed at, be the first to laugh at yourself.

Benjamin Franklin

Yo, Bro!

The *Hal* of Brotherhood

Laughter is the closest distance
between two people.

Victor Borge

I've never forgotten the teenager I sat next to on an air-plane once. It was her first time to fly, and she was a little apprehensive, to say the least. Just as we were beginning to taxi down the runway, she turned to me and asked, "Do the wings flap when we take off?"

We're all in this life together. We need each other.

And the best way to form a lasting bond with someone is through humor. People who laugh together form some of the strongest ties. Share a *Ha!* with someone—one of those deep belly laughs that go on for minutes, that keep coming back every time you replay the incident or the quip in your head—and I guarantee you'll not soon forget that person.

Man is distinguished from all other creatures by the faculty of laughter.

Joseph Addison

Laughter is the true brotherhood of man. At some time or another we've all done something that could be laughed at. Anyone who claims he hasn't is the most laughable of all.

Gene Perret

Way Different!

The *Ha!* of Men and Women

I love women. They're the best thing ever created. If they want to be like men and come down to our level, that's fine.

Mel Gibson

Men and women are different, and it's because of these differences that comedians, books, movies, and sitcoms have kept us laughing all these years. He leaves the toilet seat up; she wants it down. She hogs the blankets; he snores. She complains that he never talks; he says she won't let him get a word in edgewise. She likes to shop till he drops; he wants to watch football without interference. She sets the thermostat to "Volcano"; he sets it to "Ice Fishing." With all that potential for friction, smart couples know they need plenty of *Ha!*

I once dated the town librarian. I asked her to marry me once, and she said, "SSSShhhhhh."

Gene Perret

If a man watches three football games
in a row, he should be declared legally dead.

Erma Bombeck

A woman's mind is cleaner than a man's.
She changes it more often.

Oliver Herford

Part One: Celebrating the *Ha!*

Last week I stated that this woman was the
ugliest woman I had ever seen. I have since
been visited by her sister and now wish to
withdraw that statement.

Mark Twain

If high heels were so wonderful, men
would still be wearing them.

Sue Grafton

I DO!

The *Ha!* of Marriage

I love you more today than yesterday,
but not as much as tomorrow. Which, if my
math is correct, gives me tonight off.

Gene Perret

I read about an elderly man who was asked by a reporter for the secret to his seventy-five-year marriage. He said, "Neither one of us can hear anymore, so it makes no sense to argue."

Any couple who thinks their marriage is perfect is

probably still at their reception. Ask anyone who's been married any length of time, and he or she will undoubtedly tell you that one of the secrets to a happy and lasting marriage is a healthy sense of humor.

Laughter can make even the most irritating of habits tolerable. And whenever two people are living under the same roof, there's bound to be plenty of opportunity for aggravation. But if we don't learn to laugh about some of the frustrations of marriage, the good parts of marriage will suffer. Remember, no matter how long your list is of irritating things about your spouse, your spouse has a list too. Talk with each other about the things on those lists, work on the areas where you can improve, and have a good *Ha!* about the rest.

My mother buried three husbands—and two of them were just napping.

Rita Rudner

A man who had just finished one of those marriage books that encourage men to be the head of the home woke up the next morning and told his wife that from that moment forth, he was going to be in charge, and she would have to obey and meet his every request.

"You're going to cook a real dinner tonight, not something in the microwave, and there will also be a homemade dessert, and when I'm finished eating, you will make my bath, with bubbles, so I can relax. And after that, guess who's going to dress me and comb my hair?"

His wife said, "The funeral director."

Unknown

My wife has a slight impediment in her speech.
Every now and then she stops to breathe.

Jimmy Durante

My wife keeps complaining I never listen
to her . . . or something like that.

Bumper sticker

When my daughter-in-law (she and our son were living with us at the time) and I went away on a short trip, we asked our husbands to keep the indoor plants watered until we returned. They vowed that they would. However, by the time we returned, the plants were near death.

"Why didn't you water them like we asked?" we said.

"Well, we may have forgotten about those small ones, but look at how good the big ones look. We watered them. Are you going to say something about them?"

"Yeah. They're fake."

You know what I did before I married?
Anything I wanted to.

Henny Youngman

My wife and I were happy for twenty years.
Then we met!

Rodney Dangerfield

I was married by a judge. I should
have asked for a jury.

Groucho Marx

After about twenty years of marriage, I'm finally starting to scratch the surface of what women want. And I think the answer lies somewhere between conversation and chocolate.

Mel Gibson

Kids!
The *Ha!* of Having Children

I used to walk into a party and scan the room for attractive women. Now I look for women to hold my baby so I can eat potato salad sitting down.

Paul Reiser

The world of child rearing offers us plenty of *Ha!* Kids are great comedy material. And if you have children, you know you have to laugh just to survive. A tennis ball gets flushed down the toilet, you find a slice of pizza in your VCR, the dog gets a bath in the Easter-egg dye, the cat gets a body waxing . . . So many things can go wrong, and sometimes it seems your only options are either to laugh or to cry.

Laughter is better—at least it won't get the furniture all soggy. Which is good, since the kids have already brought the garden hose into the house and are washing down the sofa.

Electricity can be dangerous. My nephew tried to stick a penny into a plug. Whoever said a penny doesn't go far didn't see him shoot across that floor. I told him he was grounded.

Tim Allen

Have you any idea how many kids it takes to turn off one light in the kitchen? Three. It takes one to say, "What light?" and two more to say, "I didn't turn it on."

Erma Bombeck

Somewhere on this globe, every ten seconds, there is a woman giving birth to a child. She must be found and stopped.

Sam Levenson

Always be nice to your children, because they are the ones who will choose your rest home.

Phyllis Diller

Few things are more satisfying than seeing your own children have teenagers of their own.

Doug Larson

Family Fun!
The *Ha!* of Families

A good laugh is sunshine in the house.

William Makepeace Thackeray

Plenty of laughter is a sign of a healthy family. Real laughter. Belly-laugh kind of laughter. Whether it comes from watching funny movies or television shows together, whether it's the *Ha!* of sharing some family story or re-

Save 60%!

Mail today!

living an embarrassing moment, families that can laugh together tend to stay just a little bit closer than other families.

Laughter helps ease the daily stresses of family life. It takes the sting out of painful situations. It can buffer bad news or bring good news to new heights. It can be the basis for some of your best family memories. It can stop an argument dead in its tracks. It can be all the entertainment you need. It can be healing. It can bring hope. Laughter happens in the best of families.

Smartness runs in my family.
When I went to school, I was so smart
my teacher was in my class for five years.

Gracie Allen

To lose one parent may be regarded as a
misfortune; to lose both looks like carelessness.

Oscar Wilde

Me and my dad used to play tag. He'd drive.

Rodney Dangerfield

If you cannot get rid of the family skeleton,
you may as well make it dance.

George Bernard Shaw

Ties That Bind!

The *Ha!* of Extended Families

The wife's mother said, "When you're dead,
I'll dance on your grave." I said, "Good,
I'm being buried at sea."

LES DAWSON

Most of us have some people in the family whom we
think we might rather do without. The meddling
mother-in-law, the lazy brother-in-law, the embarrassing

uncle . . . whoever they are, they can really get on our nerves. So what's a person to do? Well, we could move to a deserted island and not take the cell phone with us. Or we can learn to laugh about those loved ones' irritating tendencies. Most people, since the world is running out of deserted islands, opt for meeting the situation with a sense of humor.

If it's any comfort, lots of people have had to deal with at least one irritant in his or her family line. Dysfunctional families started way back with the very first one. So if your mother-in-law is always criticizing you, if your cousin's husband is overbearing, if your extended family tree could, in your opinion, use a little pruning, laughter just might be the best (and most legal) key to survival.

As reported on an actual insurance claim form:
"I pulled away from the side of the road,
glanced at my mother-in-law, and headed over
the embankment."

Unknown

Part One: Celebrating the *Ha!*

I said to my mother-in-law, "My house is
your house." She sold it!

Henny Youngman

Mother-in-law to son-in-law:
You're about a foot from an idiot!
Son-in-law to mother-in-law:
I'm sorry. Am I crowding you?

Red Skelton, as Clem Kadiddlehopper

A family was on a trip to the Holy Land when the mother-in-law died. They went to an undertaker, who explained that the body could be shipped home, but the cost might be well over five thousand dollars. The other option was that they could bury the woman in the Holy Land for only $150.

The son-in-law of the deceased woman didn't hesitate. He said, "We'll ship her home."

The undertaker asked, "Are you sure? We can do a very nice burial here, and it would save you an awful lot of money."

The son-in-law said, "Look, some two thousand years ago, they buried a guy here, and three days later he rose from the dead. I just can't take that chance!"

Unknown

41

A man asked his prospective son-in-law, "Son, before I give you permission to marry my daughter, I need to know, can you support a family?"

The groom-to-be, a little taken aback, replied, "Well, to tell you the truth, I was just planning on supporting your daughter. All the rest of you are going to have to fend for yourselves."

Unknown

Quiet!

The *Hal* of Neighbors

My neighbor asked if he could use my lawn mower, and I told him of course he could, so long as he didn't take it out of my garden.

Eric Morecambe

Hey, neighbor! I couldn't help noticing that you put in a new privacy fence...

Ever wish you could do a personality check on your prospective neighbors before you move into the neighborhood? It would be nice, wouldn't it, just to see which ones are going to be the fun, understanding, and caring neighbors, and which will be the nitpicking, boundary-crossing, meddlesome ones. Think of all the time and trouble it would save if we knew ahead of time which people to keep at arm's length and which to embrace in friendship.

But we don't usually get this kind of advance warning. We have to get to know our neighbors the old-fashioned way—by positive or negative interaction. If it's negative (their lawn mower runs over your azaleas, their kid rides his skateboard into your freshly poured cement driveway, their daughter has band practice until 2:00 a.m., they never return the things they borrow), you'll need a healthy dose of *Ha!* Neighborly aggravations are a lot easier to handle when we look at them with a sense of humor.

neighbor, n. One whom we are commanded to love as ourselves, and who does all he knows how to make us disobedient.

Ambrose Bierce

The Bible tells us to love our neighbors, and also to love our enemies; probably because generally they are the same people.

G. K. Chesterton

A good neighbor is a fellow who smiles at you over the back fence, but doesn't climb over it.

Arthur Baer

Nothing makes you more tolerant of a neighbor's noisy party than being there.

Franklin P. Jones

Nevermore!

The *Ha!* of Dieting

You know you're getting fat when you
can pinch an inch on your forehead.

John Mendoza

Have you ever noticed that advertisers seem to know the
precise time you decide to go on a diet? It's like they save
up all their Krispy Kreme and Ben & Jerry ads for that
very moment and then start bombarding you with in-
your-face commercials featuring their way-too-delicious
products. Don't they know that it's not easy to go on a
diet in the first place? Some days it seems like the whole
world is against your losing a single pound.

"Aw, come on, it's only one chocolate éclair. What's it going to hurt?"

"There's one slice of cheesecake left. You interested?"

"Can you hold this ice-cream cone for me for a minute? If it starts to melt, go ahead and lick it."

"Hot doughnuts now!"

Temptation with a capital *T*. What's a person on a diet to do?

Have a good laugh about it all. Remember, a hearty laugh burns calories, and since it's hard to laugh and eat dessert at the same time, you're sure to lose some weight eventually. And even if you don't, you'll feel a lot better about yourself, no matter how much you happen to weigh. So go on the Humor Diet, and learn what so many others are coming to realize. Carbs aren't the enemy; discouragement and negativity are.

It's bad to suppress laughter. It goes back down and spreads to your hips.

Fred Allen

Cucumbers should be well sliced, dressed with pepper and vinegar, and then thrown out.

Samuel Johnson

Personally, I stay away from natural foods. At my age I need all the preservatives I can get.

George Burns

The Raven-ing

Once upon a diet dreary,
I lay famished, weak and weary,
Hunger pangs too fast and numerous
For my stomach to ignore.
Bathroom scale, it was just mocking.
Still, I would have eaten caulking
If somebody wasn't knocking,
Knocking at my condo door.
"Oh, be Pizza Hut!" I muttered,
Knocking at my condo door.
"Double Cheese, I'm praying for!"

I was on the Atkins Diet
Till a breadstick caused a riot.
On to Weight Watchers to try it,
Hoping I could eat some more.
But they had a rule they followed—
A whole ham could not be swallowed.
So in self-pity I wallowed,
Licking crumbs up off my floor.
Then I heard more of that knocking,
Tapping, rapping at my door,
And wondered who it could be for.

49

Part One: Celebrating the Ha!

Oh, I've dreamed of eating Twinkies,
Licking filling off my pinkies,
Scrambled eggs and sausage linkies,
Little Debbie cakes galore!
Dreamed of sourdough from 'Frisco,
Every snack sold by Nabisco,
Chocolate bars and even Crisco.
Could I last a second more?
Desperation was incoming;
I was starved down to my core!
Drat this diet evermore!

It is water I'm retaining,
That's the reason for my gaining.
And don't think that I'm complaining;
I just need to eat some more!
I love fat; I won't deny it.
Food is better when you fry it!
See a Snickers and I buy it,
Fill my cart with half the store!
All I think about is eating.
Is that a Fruit Loop on the floor?
Drat this diet ever more!

So I turned the knob and then I
Opened up the door, but when I
Saw the one who wanted in, I

Had to shut the door once more.
'Twas my trainer looking for me,
To work out she would implore me.
How I wish she'd just ignore me!
But she barged right through the door!
To the scales she dragged me screaming,
And I watched the numbers soar.
Could it be that I weighted more?

"Look at all the pounds you've packed on!
From the burgers you have macked on!
And the Ding Dongs you have snacked on!"
And you're lazy to your core!
With the accusations flying,
I assured her I was trying.
I was starving, maybe dying,
But she heard me out no more.
She just said I had to lose weight,
Then knocked my Kit Kats on the floor.
Drat that woman ever more!

Once again I vowed to diet,
But she told me to be quiet.
Exercise, I was to try it,
So I did what she implored.
I stepped back and took position.
I would stop her inquisition.

51

Part One: Celebrating the Hal

Did one leg lift in submission,
Then I kicked her out the door!
I felt great, I will admit it.
I should've exercised before!
That kind of work out I adore!

So now I'm back to eating Twinkies,
Licking filling off my pinkies;
Scrambled eggs and sausage linkies,
Little Debbie cakes galore.
I don't need no weight-loss planning.
Workout tapes I will be banning.
In the space I'll end up spanning,
I'll be happy to my core!
No more Atkins! No more South Beach!
Calories? Who's keeping score?
And I'll be hungry nevermore!

Ugh!

The *Ha!* of Exercise

I take my only exercise acting as
pallbearer at the funerals of my friends
who exercise regularly.

Mark Twain

In an attempt to get rid of cellulite on my arms, I once
tried one of those vibrator-belt contraptions. I leaned one
arm into the belt and let the belt vibrate it, then I leaned

the other arm into the belt and repeated the process. Next, I did my hips and thighs and then went on about my day. I felt pretty good that I was actually doing something about my bodily changes instead of just complaining about them.

The following morning, in front of the mirror, I couldn't help noticing that my arms looked a little different. I was hoping I'd see some changes right away, but this wasn't quite the look I was going for. All of my upper-arm fat had slid down to my elbows, leaving quite a noticeable indentation in the upper portion of the arm and creating a fat pool around my elbows. I looked like Popeye! I just stared, not sure whether I should cry or laugh. I think I did a little of both.

I made an appointment with my doctor to see what he thought about it. He examined me, then called in his partner to take a look. "How did you do this again?" he asked. I explained my experience with the vibrator belt. He shook his head in bewilderment. Apparently I was some kind of medical oddity.

I quit wearing short-sleeved shirts and basically adjusted to the fact that I had disfigured myself in the attempt to improve my looks. It's kind of like getting hit by a truck while you're jogging, or drowning during water aerobics. But there was nothing I could do about it. I was doomed to spend the rest of my life looking like I was wearing a pair of Floaties. Or so I thought.

About two years later I woke up one morning and looked in the mirror, this time to discover that all the fat had mysteriously returned to my upper arms, sort of like the swallows returning to Capistrano. It was as if the flab had just gone south for a sabbatical and had now returned to work. No one could explain why it happened or how the damage reversed itself and returned my arms to normal. So I use a lot of precaution whenever I exercise now. I've had an anchor attached to my rowing machine, I wear a helmet on my exercise bike, and I've added railings to my stairstepper. I don't use the vibrator belt anymore either. I don't think Popeye needs the competition.

I've started an exercise program. I do twenty sit-ups each morning. That may not sound like a lot, but you can only hit that snooze button so many times.

Unknown

The laziest man I ever met put
popcorn in his pancakes so they would
turn over by themselves.

W. C. Fields

I finally found the perfect gym for me.
But the staff members at Gymboree keep
making me get down off the plastic castle
and let the kids have a turn.

The word *aerobics* came about when the gym instructors got together and said, "If we're going to charge ten dollars an hour, we can't just call it Jumping Up and Down."

Rita Rudner

Happy Birthday!

The *Hal* of Aging

I've had more parts lifted than an
abandoned Mercedes.

Phyllis Diller

If we're lucky, it's going to happen to us. We're going to get older. We'll still be around long after our skin doesn't fit us anymore. If we're lucky. We're going to have hot flashes so horrible, we'll think we've discovered a new energy source. Age happens, and there isn't a lot we can do about it. So we might as well laugh. It doesn't do us any good to sit around and count wrinkles. It doesn't do us any good to dream about days gone by. Let's enjoy whatever age we happen to be, because we'll never see that age again. And if we can laugh about the body and life changes we're going through, the journey will be that much easier to take.

I don't feel old. I don't feel anything until noon. Then it's time for my nap.

Bob Hope

Part One: Celebrating the *Ha!*

An elderly man was driving down the interstate when his cell phone rang. It was his wife in a panic.

"Herman! The news just said that there's a car going the wrong way on Interstate 77. Watch out for it!"

"Heck," said Herman, "It's not just one car, sweetie. It's hundreds of them!"

Unknown

A couple of elderly friends had been meeting for lunch for years when one friend looked at the other and said, "Please excuse my memory, old friend, but right now I just can't think of your name. I know we've been friends a long time, but for the life of me, I just can't remember it. Please tell me again, what's your name?"

Taken aback because they had been friends for decades, the other friend just kind of glared at her in disbelief. Finally she said, "How soon do you need to know?"

Unknown

I tan the easy way. I just wait for my
liver spots to connect.

Part One: Celebrating the *Hal*

Little Johnny: Grandma, how old are you?
Grandma: Thirty-nine and holding.
Little Johnny: How old would you be if you let go?

As you get older you'll notice your toenails will start growing to incredible lengths. Which has its advantages. You can go swimming and spear fishing at the same time.

Except for an occasional heart attack,
I feel as young as I ever did.

Robert Benchley

Just So You Know . . .
Middle-Age Fashion Faux Pas

It's fine that people want to dress young, but despite what you may have seen on the streets, the following combinations do not go together:

- A nose ring and bifocals
- Spiked hair and bald spots
- A pierced tongue and dentures
- Miniskirts and support hose
- Ankle bracelets and corn pads
- Speedos and cellulite
- A bellybutton ring and a gall-bladder surgery scar
- Unbuttoned disco shirts and a heart monitor
- Midriff shirts and a midriff bulge
- Short shorts and varicose veins
- In-line skates and a walker

My skin doesn't fit me anymore. It's like one too
many people told me to "hang loose."

Hotels for Middle-Agers and Beyond

The Crampton Inn
Fall-a-day Inn
Hotel Vicks
The Dyeatt
The Wind'Em Hotel
Grump Towers

Driving Test for Middle-Agers and Beyond

1. How long can a left-turn signal blink before burning out?
   a. 100 miles
   b. 200 miles
   c. 500 miles
   d. The life of the car

2. When involved in a fender bender, the first thing you should do is:
   a. Wake up from your nap
   b. Put down your lipstick
   c. Put down your cell phone
   d. All of the above

3. How many donut cushions can be stacked on top of each other on the driver's seat before visibility is impaired?

   a. Two

   b. Three, if you have a sunroof

   c. Four, if you have age-related shrinkage and a sunroof

   d. Buy a convertible and use as many as you want!

4. How many trash cans can be safely dragged along behind your vehicle after you've backed over them?

   a. One

   b. One per wheel

   c. If metal, no more than two because of the spark factor

   d. I was nowhere near the trash cans, and you can't prove a thing

5. It is Sunday. What is the speed limit on a sidewalk?

   a. 30 mph

   b. 35 mph

   c. 15 mph

   d. This is a trick question. Everyone knows you're not allowed to drive on the sidewalks on weekends.

6. Windshield wipers should be used:
   a. Whenever it's raining
   b. Whenever it's raining or sleeting
   c. Whenever it's raining, sleeting, or snowing
   d. Continuously, no matter what the weather

7. A red light means:
   a. Come to a full and complete stop
   b. Ease into the intersection approximately ten feet, then stop
   c. Drive through the intersection at normal speed and wave
   d. Hit brakes, go, hit brakes again, go, and continue this sequence until you've crossed the intersection, then stop and ask yourself three questions: Did I just go through a red light? Was there a cop around? Am I driving?

8. If a truck is honking behind you as you're traveling down a steep incline, you should:
   a. Let him push you. You could save a fortune on gas
   b. Immediately apply your brakes and see what he wants
   c. Wait until the next truck stop, follow him off the exit, and let the air out of his tires for tailgating and stressing you like that
   d. All of the above

9. Side mirrors are for:
   a. Tweezing your chin hairs
   b. Putting on lipstick, if the inside mirror is foggy
   c. Using as bumpers and distance gauges when parking in tight spaces
   d. Hanging bags of groceries when the trunk is full

10. Accidents should be reported to your insurance company:
    a. Within three days
    b. Within one week
    c. Within one month
    d. Daily

11. A raised median means:
    a. Your personal left-turn lane
    b. A scenic viewpoint
    c. Camping is permitted after dusk
    d. All of the above

12. If while driving on the interstate you happen to see a chair in your lane that has obviously fallen off a delivery truck, you should:
    a. Stop and check to see if it's a recliner
    b. Report it to the local highway patrol, then see if it's a recliner

c. Pick it up and keep your eyes open for the matching chair farther down the road

d. Drive over it and spend the rest of the afternoon trying to figure out what in the world kind of roadkill that was

In the end, it's not the years in your life that count. It's the life in your years.

Abraham Lincoln

Not So Well!

The *Hal* of the Medical World

First the doctor told me the good news: I was going to have a disease named after me.

Steve Martin

Doctors are human, just like the rest of us. They have days when their bedside manner isn't the best. They might even make some pretty big mistakes. Just ask someone who's had the wrong body part removed. Even if the body part that was removed was a less-expensive procedure, that person probably wasn't too happy about the error. Still, when these sorts of things happen, I'm often amazed at the attitudes of some of the people involved. Frequently they have a take on the situation that is far more understanding than many of us might.

"Well, what are you going to do? These things happen."

"I guess I didn't need that spleen anyway."

"I look at it this way: next time he'll know exactly where that organ is."

Even with the occasional mistake (and they are rare), where would we be without the hard-working, dedicated members of the medical field? How many times have they literally saved our lives? How many hours of sleep have we caused them to lose while they treated our late-night injuries or illnesses? Or those of our children?

So the next time a doctor shows a little bit of his or her human side, try accepting some of those fallibilities with a sense of humor. Major blunders by inept physicians are a different issue. They, of course, should be addressed and dealt with through the proper channels. But, all those times when we could lighten up and be more understanding of those in the medical field, we should do it. Sometimes even doctors need to be reminded that laughter is the best medicine.

Doctor to patient: I have good news
and bad news. The good news is that
you are not a hypochondriac.

Unknown

I told my doctor that everyone hates me.
He said, "Don't be ridiculous. Everyone
doesn't know you yet."

Rodney Dangerfield

Late one night a mountain man's wife went into labor, and the doctor was called out to his run-down old cabin in the Blue Ridge Mountains for the delivery. There was no electricity at the homestead, so the doctor handed the daddy-to-be a lantern and told him, "Here. Hold this high so I can see what I am doing."

It wasn't long before a beautiful baby boy was brought into the world. The new father put the lantern down and reached for his son, but the doctor said, "Whoa, hold on a minute there. Get that lantern back up. I think there's another one coming."

Sure enough, a few minutes later the doctor delivered a baby girl.

The new daddy was ecstatic, but once again the doctor told him not to put down the lantern. "I think there's yet another one coming," he said.

The doctor was right again. Within a few minutes he delivered a third baby!

"That's three of 'em!" exclaimed the overwhelmed father.

"Yep, but I wouldn't be in a hurry to put down that lantern. I think I see another one coming!" the doctor said.

The mountain man scratched his head in bewilderment, then asked, "You reckon it's the light that's attractin' 'em, Doc?"

Unknown

The colder the x-ray table, the more of your body is required to be on it.

Steven Wright

I have always believed that a good laugh was good for both the mental and physical digestion.

Abraham Lincoln

Get to Work!

The *Ha!* of the Workplace

A meeting is a gathering of important people who singly can do nothing, but together can decide that nothing can be done.

Fred Allen

If not for humor in the workplace, there would probably be a lot more hostage situations. Humor helps to make a long day shorter. It can diffuse tension and help take the sting out of the daily antics of that annoying coworker or that overbearing boss.

Part One: Celebrating the Hal

It's good to keep in mind, however, that sometimes work humor can be caustic and meanspirited, and if that's the case, it's unhealthy and will likely cause more problems than it solves. But when used as a harmless stress reliever, humor can be powerful. And let's face it, if we have to spend eight hours a day with these people, day in and day out, we might as well share a laugh or two along the way.

I always arrive late at the office,
but I make up for it by leaving early.

Charles Lamb

A lot of fellows nowadays have a BA, MD, or PhD. Unfortunately, they don't have a JOB.

Fats Domino

You Might Be a Workaholic If . . .

- You've ever used Maalox as gravy
- You consider a walk to Kinko's your evening exercise
- Your home movies have the stock market report crawling across the bottom of the screen
- Your laptop has seen more of your lap than your children have
- While being wheeled into the emergency room on a stretcher, you've handed a file to the nurse and said, "Here, fax this"
- The only family pictures with you in them are the ones where your image has been digitally added
- The last time you stopped and smelled the roses was when you fell asleep at the wheel and crashed into a flower shop
- You play lullabies to your children using the tones on your cell phone and beeper
- You've been known to use your computer mouse pad as a pillow
- While showing off your new baby's hospital picture to some friends, your spouse reminds you that your baby just turned seventeen

YUCK!

The *Ha!* of Housekeeping

Housework can't kill you, but why
take a chance?

Phyllis Diller

Dust bunnies do NOT bite! You have to come up with a better excuse than that!

I'm just not into housework. I like a clean house; I just don't like cleaning house. Heloise and I could never be close friends, because she would not understand why my washing machine has a mildew cycle. I've come to terms with that.

There is the other extreme though. People who alphabetize their soup cans have their own issues to deal with.

The best way to be, I suppose, is somewhere in the middle. Keep the floors clean enough to eat off of, but have enough food down there to make it worth your while. And keep a good sense of humor about it.

Nature abhors a vacuum. And so do I.

Anne Gibbons

For years my family thought mold was a frosting.

You Know It's Time to Clean House When . . .

- The last clean newspaper in the bottom of your parrot's cage has the headline, "Capone Captured!"
- You haven't given your dog a bath in so long, the only thing he'll sit up and beg for is deodorant
- Buzzards are circling your trash cans . . . the ones *inside* the house
- Your mountain of dirty laundry is so high, you could ski down it
- Your closet is so cluttered, the moths need special clearance to land
- You open your refrigerator door, and a four-month-old chicken-salad sandwich climbs out and walks itself to the garbage disposal
- The muffin that rolled under your bed two months ago now has enough hair to French braid
- You can't walk barefoot on the floor without getting a paper cut

- You don't need a Roach Motel, you need a Roach Convention Center
- The floral pattern on your sheets starts taking root
- There are so many empty soda cans on your floor, the neighbors mistake your house for a recycling center
- Your bed has seen more cookie crumbs than a Nabisco factory
- You fluff your pillow and three bats fly out

Amen!

The *Ha!* of Church

The secret of a good sermon is to have a good beginning and a good ending, then having the two as close together as possible.

George Burns

Don't take it personally, Reverend. Sometimes at home he falls asleep when we're just saying grace.

Some people believe church life shouldn't have any laughs, but I don't understand that kind of thinking. If God didn't think laughter was important, why did He create us with the equipment to laugh? Besides, laughter can be a pretty powerful way to present a biblical truth, as countless preachers, priests, evangelists, and Christian comedians have discovered. And if laughter is healthy and good outside of the church, it stands to reason that it's healthy and good inside the church too.

And plenty of comedy happens in church. If you don't believe me, just join one. The dynamics of church life are ripe for humor. That's because the people sitting in the pews, the pastor behind the pulpit, the choir directors and members, the church board . . . not a single one of them is perfect. They're going to make mistakes, and sometimes those mistakes will bring plenty of *Ha!* along with them.

And like the Good Book says, *Ha!* is good medicine.

The cheerful heart has a continual feast.

Proverbs 15:15

After attending the christening ceremony of his baby brother, little Johnny sat in the backseat of his car and cried all the way home. His father had asked him three times what was wrong, but each time he wouldn't answer. Finally the boy replied, "That priest said he wanted us brought up in a Christian home. But I want to stay with you guys!"

Unknown

Part One: Celebrating the Ha!

As the preacher's sermon dragged on and on, a little girl started fidgeting in the pew. She tried her best to keep still, but she just couldn't. The preacher had taken up every ounce of her patience. Finally she leaned over to her mother and whispered, "Mommy, if we give him the money now, will he let us go?"

Unknown

After one Sunday-morning service, the pastor noticed a little boy in the foyer of the church staring up at a large memorial that hung on the wall. It had names listed on it and several small American flags bordering it. The young lad seemed to be intensely studying it, so the pastor said, "Nice, huh?"

The boy said, "Yeah, but what is it, pastor?"

The pastor said proudly, "It's a memorial to all the brave young men and women who died in the service."

They both stood there staring at the names, somberly. Then the young lad asked, in an almost whisper, "Which service, pastor? The nine o'clock or the ten-thirty?"

Unknown

Honk, Honk!

The *Ha!* of the Road

When buying a used car, punch the buttons on the radio. If all the stations are rock and roll, there's a good chance the transmission is shot.

Larry Lujack

Road rage. Carjackings. Speeders. Tailgaters. Drivers who cut you off. Drivers putting on makeup. Drivers tending to unruly children in the backseat. Eighteen-wheelers.

Traffic jams. Cars with the left-turn signal blinking for the last two hundred miles. Drivers swerving out of their lanes while dialing their cell phones. The price of gas. Husbands who won't ask directions. Wives who won't say they need to use the gas-station facilities until you've filled up and are pulling back onto the interstate. Traffic cops meeting their ticket quota. Snipers. Flat tires. Blown transmissions. Overheated radiators.

There doesn't seem to be a lot to laugh about out there on the road these days. But if you look hard enough, you can find humor. That could be the whole reason bumper stickers were invented in the first place. Maybe some guy was stuck in traffic and said to himself, *I could sure use a good laugh right now*. We all could use a good laugh when we find ourselves surrounded by ill-tempered drivers and frustrating delays on the highway.

I couldn't repair your brakes,
so I made your horn louder.

Steven Wright

Bumper Stickers as Seen on the Road:

- Forget about world peace . . . visualize using your turn signal!
- Suburbia: where they cut down all the trees and then name streets after them.
- He who hesitates is not only lost but miles from the next exit.
- How many roads must a man travel down before he admits he is lost?
- Boldly Going Nowhere
- Due to budget cuts, light at end of tunnel will be out.

Comic Relief!

The *Ha!* of Life

Laugh and the world laughs with you.
Cry and you simply get wet.

Cliff Thomas

Comedians know that the best comedy comes from real life. Truth—it doesn't get any funnier than that.

Writers couldn't make up all of the comic relief life hands us on a regular basis. It always seems so perfectly timed too. Right in the middle of that stressful business meeting or that formal dinner we're regretting having RSVP'd for, right when we're about to lose that argument with a spouse, comic relief comes along, and all the tension goes away. Suddenly the situation is tolerable again. Those "knuckleheads" at the business meeting are now laughing with us and don't seem nearly as annoying as they once did. That formal dinner is a lot more relaxed now that we've loosened up with a chuckle or two. In fact, we're even enjoying ourselves. And that disagreement with your spouse doesn't seem nearly as important to win, does it, now that the two of you are laughing together?

We can count on life giving us plenty of *Ha!* moments. It's up to us to catch them. And we should, because they'll make our journey so much easier.

Does God have a sense of humor?
He must have if He created us.

Jackie Gleason

We are all here for a spell.
Get all the laughs you can.

Will Rogers

Oh My!

The *Hal* of Difficult People

I like long walks, especially when they are taken by people who annoy me.

Fred Allen

Ever find yourself just standing there after someone has launched a verbal barb at you, and you can't think of a single thing to say in return until two o'clock the following afternoon, but by then no one is around to hear how witty your comeback is? Difficult people usually catch us off guard. I think that's their strategy. They know we're not as practiced at delivering these jabs, so the surprise attack works in their favor. Often they've been delivering them for most of their lives.

Difficult people are sometimes like hurricanes. Just after we get battered by one storm, we get lulled into relaxing, thinking they're not as difficult as they once seemed, only to let down our guard and after the calm of the eye passes over, we get hit again.

So how can we laugh when a difficult person is making life miserable? What good is a *Ha!* when what we really feel like saying is *Ouch!*

The simple fact is this: the difficult people in our lives might never change. They might remain their hurting, manipulative-behavior selves for the rest of their lives. The only person we truly have the power to change is ourselves. We can change how we view these people, or we can change how we react to them. Or we might just have to maintain some distance. Sometimes bullies just want to know that they've made us uncomfortable. If we don't give that to them, if we laugh off their latest troublemaking, we're making the change in us—again, the only person we can change. And then we get the final *Ha!*

HERE LIES
A VERY
DIFFICULT
PERSON

Part One: Celebrating the *Hal*

The trouble with her is that she lacks
the power of conversation but not
the power of speech.

George Bernard Shaw

He was a great patriot, a humanitarian,
a loyal friend; provided, of course,
he really is dead.

Voltaire

The problem with the gene pool is
that there is no lifeguard.

Steven Wright

Men are apt to offend ('tis true) where they find
most goodness to forgive.

William Congreve

Oh Boy!

The *Hal* of Vacations

It always rains on tents. Rainstorms will travel thousands of miles, against prevailing winds, for the opportunity to rain on a tent.

Dave Barry

How much farther?

We're told we need them. Many employers force us to take them. But if vacations are supposed to be so good for us, why do they cause us so much stress?

Vacations are a time of lost wallets and lost patience. Of kids arguing in the backseat over who is crowding whom. Vacations are about rainstorms the likes of which haven't been seen since Noah, and the dark clouds seem to be following only your minivan. They're about over-priced souvenirs and hotels that look nothing like they did in the brochures.

But vacations can also be about family bonding. (What else is there to do when you're stranded on the side of the road with a blown transmission?) And they're about making memories. If we wait for the perfect vacation to make a memory, it might never come. Besides, sometimes the memories we think are the worst end up being the ones we remember with the most laughter. They might even turn out to be the family favorites!

So just as you would schedule plenty of rest stops along your vacation route, be sure to schedule in some laugh breaks too. And no matter what, enjoy your time together.

A travel agent told me I could spend six nights in Puerto Rico. No days, just nights. I said to him, "What will I do with myself days?" He said, "Do whatever you want, just keep out of Puerto Rico."

Rodney Dangerfield

I walked up to a tourist information booth. I asked them to tell me about a couple people who were here last year.

Steven Wright

You Know It's Time to Go Home When . . .

- Your car's radiator is keeping a more regular eruption schedule than Old Faithful
- You can't remember at which rest stop you left your hat, your sunglasses, and two of your children
- The magnetic pull of all your souvenir refrigerator magnets is starting to suck the bumpers off of passing cars
- After 487 tries you still haven't figured out how to refold your map

- You don't know which is getting balder—your tires or the numbers on your American Express card
- There's so much dirty laundry in your suitcases, buzzards are starting to circle your luggage rack
- You're actually starting to like the hot dogs at gas-station minimarts
- You're finding the last of your cash is harder to hold on to than one of those tiny bars of motel soap

Part One: Celebrating the *Ha!*

- You've smiled and said "cheese" so often, you feel like a Kraft salesman
- Every time you open the trunk of your car, other tourists mistake it for a roadside souvenir stand and start shopping
- The mosquitoes are taking bigger bites out of you than the price of gas
- Your car has gathered more dust than your kids' schoolbooks
- You don't know which has more new bulges—your luggage or your waist
- That irritating "Are we there yet?" whining is getting totally out of hand, but no matter how hard they try, your kids can't get you to stop doing it

Vote!

The *Ha!* of Politics

There's no trick to being a humorist when you have the whole government working for you.

Will Rogers

If it weren't for all the politicians, comedy writers and comedians would lose a good portion of their material. Politics provide great fodder for humor. This candidate says this, that candidate says that, this political party stands for this ridiculous platform, that political party stands for that ridiculous platform. Who's right? Who knows? But one thing's for sure, it all gives us more to laugh about.

Part One: Celebrating the *Hal*

I have come to the conclusion that politics is too serious a matter to be left to the politicians.

Charles de Gaulle

An ambassador is a person who having failed to secure an office from the people is given one by the Administration on condition that he leave the country.

Ambrose Bierce

Politics is the art of looking for trouble, finding it whether it exists or not, diagnosing it incorrectly, and applying the wrong remedy.

Ernest Benn

Too bad that all the people who know how to run the country are busy running taxicabs or cutting hair.

George Burns

A politician is someone who divides his time
between running for office and running for cover.

Gene Perret

Touchdown!

The *Ha!* of Sports and Entertainment

I find television very educating. Every time somebody turns on the set, I go into the other room and read a book.

Groucho Marx

The worlds of sports and entertainment can provide us with plenty of *Ha!* Just watch a bloopers show, and you'll know what I mean. Plays are bungled, the words to songs or scripts are forgotten or misspoken, there are clothing malfunctions, and lots of other embarrassing moments are caught on tape.

When we see that our favorite sports star or celebrity

makes a major faux pas, it makes us feel a little better about ourselves, doesn't it? It reminds us that we don't have to be perfect. It assures us that we all make our share of mistakes in life, and it helps us to go a little easier on ourselves. Some time or other, the *Ha!* happens to us all.

People are always asking me when I'm going to retire. Why should I? I've got it two ways—I'm still making movies and I'm a senior citizen, so I can see myself at half-price.

George Burns

It's good sportsmanship to not pick up lost golf balls while they are still rolling.

Mark Twain

Past Due!

The *Ha!* of Finances

Money doesn't make you happy. I now have $50 million, but I was just as happy when I had $48 million.

Arnold Schwarzenegger

It's only money. But we often fall into the trap of thinking that if we only had a little more, all our problems would disappear. That isn't true. A lot of our problems might disappear, but then we'd just have new problems.

So the next time your mailbox is full of "past due," "overdue," "Hey, loser, did you forget about us?" notes, try a little *Ha!* therapy. It won't pay the bills, but it'll make paying them a lot less painful.

Money frees you from doing things you dislike. Since I dislike doing nearly everything, money is handy.

Groucho Marx

I used to sell furniture for a living. The trouble was, it was my own.

Les Dawson

Why pay a dollar for a bookmark? Why not use the dollar for a bookmark?

Steven Spielberg

I want my children to have all the things I couldn't afford. Then I want to move in with them.

Phyllis Diller

You Know You're Financially Challenged When . . .

- You check into a hotel because all the towels at home are dirty (and you need more shampoo anyway)
- You buy an item you don't need because the rebate makes it too good of a bargain to pass up . . . then you never mail in the rebate
- Your retirement stock has taken so many dives, it could qualify for the Olympic swim team
- The only bond you own is made by Elmer's
- Your accountant sends you sympathy cards
- You ask a Girl Scout for a payment plan on your cookie order
- If all your credit cards were laid end to end, you still couldn't use any of them
- Your balance sheet has vertigo
- At your house the tooth fairy leaves IOUs
- You do more praying at the ATM than at church

I've got all the money I'll ever need if I die by
four o'clock this afternoon.

Henny Youngman

The Power of *Ha!*

Ha! Power

Against the assault of laughter,
nothing can stand.

Mark Twain

uh...uh... a guy walks into a doctor's office...

The punch line! Quickly!

Laughter can diffuse a tense situation, erase misunderstandings, heal hurt feelings, repair fractured relationships, mend broken hearts, calm frazzled nerves, instigate social connections, deepen friendships, change the hearts of enemies, and so much more. Laughter is one of the most powerful and underutilized weapons known to man. I wonder how many prescriptions could be thrown away, wars cancelled, feuds ended, and marriages restored if only laughter were applied daily.

You can't stay mad at somebody
who makes you laugh.

Jay Leno

If you lose the power to laugh, you lose
the power to think.

Clarence Darrow

Part Two: The Power of *Ha!*

Laughter gives us distance. It allows us
to step back from an event, deal with it,
and then move on.

Bob Newhart

A good laugh heals a lot of hurts.

Madeleine L'Engle

Ha! Journey

Perhaps I know why it is man alone who laughs: he alone suffers so deeply that he had to invent laughter.

Friedrich Nietzsche

If you've been at this "living" thing for any length of time at all, you know by now that the journey can at times get a little harrowing. We don't always get the road conditions we want. Often there are plenty of obstacles along the way. There's a good chance, though, that the path will

Part Two: The Power of *Ha!*

lead us exactly where we wanted to go, and we'll be better for the trouble; but going through some of these experiences can be challenging, to say the least. That's why it's important to remember to pack our sense of humor for our trek through life. Then, whatever comes our way, we'll be able to take it in stride. We'll have a good *Ha!* in spite of it all.

A person without a sense of humor
is like a wagon without springs. It's jolted
by every pebble in the road.

Henry Ward Beecher

Humor is the great thing, the saving thing.
The minute it crops up,
all our irritation and resentments slip away,
and a sunny spirit takes their place.

Mark Twain

The robbed that smiles,
steals something from the thief.

William Shakespeare

Part Two: The Power of *Ha!*

Laugh to Cope

Were it not for my little jokes, I could not bear the burdens of this office.

Abraham Lincoln

Bad news is always a little easier to swallow if there's a bit of good news to go with it. Even lectures and sermons go down a little easier if they're sprinkled with some funny anecdotes. Laughter is that spoonful of sugar that will help the medicine go down and helps us to cope. And with laughter there's no maximum dosage per day. We can laugh as often as we need to. We can even take as much of it as we want at once. No need to worry about overdosing on the stuff. Laughter is completely safe and has no negative side effects—only positive ones.

Lawyer: I have some good news and some bad news.

Client: Well, give me the bad news first.

Lawyer: The bad news is that the DNA tests showed that it was your blood they found all over the crime scene.

Client: Oh no! I'm ruined! What's the good news?

Lawyer: The good news is your cholesterol is down to 130!

Unknown

Part Two: The Power of *Hal*

Laugh to Heal

To truly laugh, you must be able to
take your pain and play with it!

Charlie Chaplin

Comedians know that a passage of time may be neces-
sary before any humor can be seen in certain situations.
That's why they time their material accordingly and wait
until people are ready to laugh again. But they know that
day will come. They've seen it happen often enough to
know that after a national or personal tragedy, the time
will come when, because of the enormous stress people

124

have been through, they'll be in dire need of a little comic relief. And when the time is right, comedians will be more than happy to provide it. Why? To make light of a serious situation? No. It's to help in the recovery process. When laughter begins again, it means the healing has also begun.

He will yet fill your mouth with laugher and
your lips with shouts of joy.

Job 8:21

Always laugh when you can.
It is cheap medicine.

Lord Byron

Laugh to Love

If you have only one smile in you,
give it to the people you love.

Maya Angelou

The easiest people to laugh with are those we love. Why? Because it usually requires very little setup. When everyone in the group remembers a certain humorous incident, the mere mention of a key word or two will conjure up a comical memory.

It's also comfortable to laugh with those we love. We don't have to worry about how loud we guffaw, whether we snort as we laugh, whether we inhale milk and nearly choke as we cackle, or whatever other little things we might do. We're free to laugh however we want to. When we're with loved ones, they'll understand.

Laughing with friends and family—does life get any better than that?

We cannot really love anybody with whom we never laugh.

Agnes Repplier

It is one of the blessings of old friends that you can afford to be stupid with them.

Ralph Waldo Emerson

The Last Laugh!

Nobody ever died of laughter.

Max Beerbohm

I met a doctor who told me that while she was visiting an elderly patient in the hospital, she was attempting to explain that they would be transferring the patient to a convalescent hospital. Being new to the area, however, the doctor got the name of the Oakdale Convalescent Home confused with the Oak Grove Cemetery.

Imagine the patient's surprise when the doctor said, "You'll be going to Oak Grove."

"But I don't want to go to Oak Grove," the elderly woman protested.

"I'm sorry, but you have to go to Oak Grove."

"But I don't want to go there," the poor woman pleaded with every ounce of strength she had left.

"I'm the doctor, and I'm going to be sending you there in a day and a half."

Luckily, the doctor realized the mistake and changed the transfer orders.

We may not know the time or place, but none of us, as Hank Williams Jr. said, are going to "get out of this world alive." As a comedy writer I've often wondered if I would go in some bizarre way. Like, will my loved ones have to say, "We told her not to take her computer into the bathtub with her, but she just mumbled something about a deadline, hit the wrong button, and deleted herself. We tried to save her as a text file, but it was too late."

However we go, one thing is certain: we are going to go. That's why we have to enjoy our lives now. Not tomorrow. We have to live with the realization that any moment might be our last one. Why, just the other night I received this e-mail: "With all the sadness and trauma going on in the world, it is worth reflecting on the death of a very important person, which almost went unnoticed last week. Larry LaPrise, the man who wrote 'The Hokey Pokey,' died peacefully at the age of eighty-three. The most traumatic part for his family was getting him into the coffin. They put his left leg in, and then the trouble started."

Laughter—get everything you can out of it . . . all the way to the end.

Either he's dead, or my watch has stopped.

Groucho Marx

He wasn't paranoid; they really were after him.

Epitaph

Health nuts are going to feel stupid someday,
lying in hospitals dying of nothing.

Redd Foxx

Part Two: The Power of *Hal*

If you die in an elevator,
be sure to push the Up button.

Sam Levenson

The reports of my death have been
greatly exaggerated.

Mark Twain

Just Laugh!

Start every day off with a smile
and get it over with.

W. C. Fields

Being miserable won't add a single day to our lives. Neither will being negative, grumpy, or irritated, or getting even, or insisting on always being right. None of that will stretch our lives a single day, hour, or minute longer. What all that will do, though, is keep us from enjoying what time we have. If we're waiting for our lives to be perfect before we can give ourselves permission to laugh, we could be waiting a long time. Life isn't perfect. No one's life is. So why not get the most out of your day, problem filled as it may be, by packing it full of laughter too? And if it gets too crowded, let a few of the problems go. But whatever you do, don't let go of your joy.

Abraham Lincoln once said, "Most people are about as happy as they make up their minds to be." He was right.

It's your life. Get every last laugh you can!

Laughter is an instant vacation.

Milton Berle

Only if we are secure in our beliefs can we see
the comical side of the universe.

Flannery O'Connor

Part Two: The Power of *Ha!*

The most wasted of all days is that in which we have not laughed.

Sebastien-Roch Nicolas de Chamfort

humor for the **lighter** side of life

Bring a gift of laughter,
sing yourselves into his presence.

Psalm 100:2 The Message